An Evening With
Abraham Lincoln

Parson's Porch Books

An Evening With Abraham Lincoln

ISBN: Softcover 978-1-960326-03-4

Copyright © 2023 by Don Germano

Parson's Porch Books is an imprint of Parson's Porch & Company (PP&C) in Cleveland, Tennessee. PP&C is an innovative organization which raises money by publishing books of noted authors, representing all genres. Its face and voice is **David Russell Tullock** (dtullock@parsonsporch.com).

Parson's Porch & Company *turns books into bread & milk* by sharing its profits with the poor.

www.parsonsporch.com

An Evening With

Abraham Lincoln

To

Sara Mac

My wife and friend of over 60 years.

Introduction

This book was inspired by my portrayal of Abraham Lincoln given on numerous occasions over the years at churches, schools, civic groups, and clubs.

The setting for this, **"An Evening with Abraham Lincoln,"** is in the office of the President of the United States in the White House in late December of 1863. All of the facts and stories depicted herein are true. Most of the dialogue and words are Lincoln's own.

Since the beginning of the great Civil War in April of 1861 with the firing upon Fort Sumter, the North had suffered a number of defeats, and Federal losses had been high. But things had begun to turn around by the middle of 1863, and the North had begun to see a number of victories by the end of that year at Gettysburg, Vicksburg, and at Chattanooga.

But here, in the quiet solitude of his office, before a small gathering of friends and well - wishers, Abraham Lincoln relaxes and reflects a little on his rise in politics to be elected President of the United State, some of the problems he has encountered in the Office of President, portions of some of his memorable speeches, as well as just some events and antidotes that have come to his mind and to which he feels like sharing.

Join him now as he shares his evening, and some memories and concerns with you!

A Lincoln

An Evening With Abraham Lincoln

Good evening! Didn't know you were here, but I'm glad you came! Almost everyone who comes to see me these days, come seeking some office or some special privilege or favor, so it's good to have someone to visit that I can just talk to! Much has been on my mind lately! This war has been on my mind! When this war began, almost all my advisors said this war would last no more than three months. We're now approaching three years, and the war goes on, and the killing and the dying goes on! We're fighting this war to preserve the nation, but sometimes I wonder if, by the time this war ends, with all this killing and dying, if there will be anybody left to enjoy this nation!

This Office of the President is a lonely and most difficult job! Sometimes I wonder why anyone would ever seek to be elected to such an office. Just the other day, a friend of mine from Springfield asked me how it felt to be President of the United States. I reminded him of the man who had been tarred and feathered and ridden out of town on a rail. When someone from the crowd shouted out and asked him how he liked it, he said, "Well, if it wasn't for the honor of the thing, I'd much rather have walked!"

Just the other day, I was thinking of my own beginnings in politics. After eight years in the State Legislature, and a couple of years serving in the Lower House of Congress, I decided, a little over five years ago, to make my own run for the Senate seat being held by Senator Stephen A. Douglas[1] of Illinois. "The Judge," as I called Senator Douglas, had been in the Senate for about eleven years. He was a man of great ability, with a magnificent speaking voice, and was generally regarded as a certain Presidential candidate in 1860. But I differed from the Judge on the issue of slavery. I had joined the Republicans who wished to exclude slavery from the territories. I launched my campaign with a speech[2] to the State Convention of the Republican Party, there in Springfield, in June of 1858:

"Mr. President, Gentlemen of the convention, a house divided against itself cannot stand! I believe this government cannot endure permanently half slave and half free. I do not expect the Union to be dissolved. I do not expect the house to fall! But I do expect that it will cease to be divided. It will become all one thing, or all the other!"

Well, within a month's time, Senator Douglas met my challenge, and we began a series of debates.[3] My own high-pitched voice was quite a contrast to the booming voice of the Judge, as was my stile! Oh, I would generally ride alone into town on a wagon. The Judge had a splendid entourage and would generally ride from town to town in his private railway car with banners and brass bands!

"I will say here that I have no purpose, directly or indirectly, to interfere with the institution of slavery in the States where it now exists. I believe I have no lawful right to do so, and I have no inclination to do so. But notwithstanding all this, I hold, that there is no reason in the world why the Negro is not entitled to all the natural rights enumerated in the Declaration of Independence, the right to life, liberty, and the pursuit of happiness. I hold, that he is as much entitled to these, as the white man!"

Well, in the end, I lost my election with Senator Douglas, by a narrow margin, but I did acquire some national recognition, and I was surprised that within a year's time, I too was being talked of as a Presidential candidate. I recall, that during the debates, my law partner, Billy Herndon[4], had predicted that the Republicans would eventually make me President! I never took him serious though! Nevertheless, it was in May of 1860 that the National Convention of the Republican Party, there in Chicago, did on its third ballot, nominate me as its candidate for President of the United States.

Shortly before the election, I received a letter from Grace Bedell[5], an eleven-year-old girl from New York. She suggested I grow a beard, said I'd look a great deal better since my face was so thin, that all the ladies liked the whiskers and that they would tease their husbands into voting for me! Well, I took her advice!

Following my election, I left by train from Springfield for Washington. A large crowd of friends had gathered there at the train station in the rain to say "goodbye." From the back of that train, I spoke[6] to these, my neighbors:

"My friends! No one, not in my situation, can appreciate my feeling of sadness at this parting. To this place, and to the kindness of these people, I owe everything! I now leave not knowing when, or whether ever I may return, with a task before me even greater than that which rested on (George) Washington! Without the assistance of that Divine Being that attended him, I cannot succeed! With that assistance, I cannot fail! Trusting in Him, who may go with me, and be with you, and be everywhere for good, let us confidently hope that all may yet be well! To His care commending you, as I hope in your prayers you will commend me, I bid you all an affectionate farewell!"

From the date of my election to the date of my inauguration, on March 4, 1861, seven Southern States had seceded from the Union. In my inaugural address as the 16th President of the United States, I appealed to these, my Southern friends:

"In your hands, my fellow dissatisfied countrymen, and not in mine, rest the momentous issue of Civil War! We are not enemies, but friends! Though patients may have strained, it must not break our bonds of affection!"

That evening, following the Inauguration Ball, I was handed a letter that said Fort Sumter was in great danger. A little over a month later, the South had fired on Fort Sumter, and I, with heavy heart, but determined to do my duty, issued a call and a proclamation for 75,000 troops to meet this crisis, and to preserve, protect, and defend the Constitution, and to save the Union! The Civil War had begun!

From the time this war began. I had trouble with my generals. I must admit that I never had much military training myself. In fact, my only military experience was a three-month stint, some thirty or so years ago, in a militia company in Northern Illinois. We were there to protect the settlers against hostile Indians. Never did see any hostile Indians, although I did survive a great many bloody battles with the mosquitoes! But you know, you don't have to be a military genius to figure this thing out! For just as a horse can't win a race by staying in the barn, an army can't win a war unless it pursues and defeats the other side. I don't know why my generals couldn't see this!

Now General McClellan[7] was a good officer. He was thought of highly by his men and his fellow officers had great confidence in his ability. But General McClellan had the "slows"! I couldn't push him into action. Throughout the winters of '61 and '62 I kept asking, "Why doesn't McClellan move with his army? How can we get him to fight?" Oh, I know that Providence, with favoring earth and sky, was beckoning our army on. But General McClellan, I suppose, knew his business, and had good reasons for disregarding these hints of Providence. Oh, he would build barriers, barricades, and entrenchments, was constantly asking for more guns, more shoes, and more canons. But while the good General was taking some time off visiting his family in Philadelphia, the hard riding J.E.B. Stuart[8], wearing gold spurs, a plum in his hat and singing in the rain, carried his Confederate forces across the Potomac River there and on up into

Chambersburg, Pennsylvania[9]. There he took five hundred horses, Federal uniforms, and all the food and clothing they could carry away! Camped his men right there in the city streets! Then moving his men back around to join General Lee, Stuart went around McClellan's army for the second time that year. Well, when I was a boy, we used to play a game called, "Three times around and you're out!" Well, Stuart has been around McClellan twice! I decided, then and there, that if General McClellan permitted Lee's army to pass over the Blue Ridge a third time and place himself between Richmond and the Army of the Potomac, I'd remove him! I guess it was in November of last year that I got the news that General Lee's army had reached Culpepper Courthouse after safely retreating there from the battles at Sharpsburg and Antietam. And I was upset with McClellan for his caution and his failure to pursue Lee. So, I sent a letter to General McClellan relieving him of command of the Army of the Potomac and ordering him to turn over command to General Burnside!

Now we didn't get into this war to put down slavery but to put the flag back. Nevertheless, after Bull Run and a number of other battles over the first two years of the war, it looked to me like we were losing this war and I began to look upon emancipation as a military necessity in order to preserve the Union. But I must admit that I always thought slavery[10] was wrong! If slavery is not wrong, nothing is wrong! I do not remember a time when I did not so think and feel! For just as I would not be a slave, so I would not be a

14

master! This expresses my idea of democracy. Anything that differs from this to the extent that there is a difference, is no democracy! So, it was on New Year's Day, during a reception, I slipped away from the crowd, made my way back here to my office, where, with a few selected members of my Cabinet and a few other dignitaries, I signed this Emancipation Proclamation[11] freeing the slaves. Ordinarily, I would sign my name, "A. Lincoln," but on this occasion, as I put my pen to the paper, I carefully wrote out my name in full, "Abraham Lincoln"! I knew, that if I was ever going to be remembered in history, it would be for this act!

Oh, I see its almost 12:00. Every day at noon I order the doors open and all those waiting outside come rushing in. Some come just to shake my hand. Most come seeking some office or some special privilege or favor. One by one though, they'll make their wants known!

"Well, friend, what can I do for you?"

Early this year a gentleman had come to see me to obtain a safe conduct pass to go to Richmond. I told him, "Sir, the Confederates don't seem to want to honor my passes. In fact, over the past two years I have issued 250,000 passes to the men of our army to go to Richmond, not one has gotten then yet! But if you can get there with my pass, you shall have it!"

I had heard of a widow woman from Tennessee who had gone to see Secretary Stanton[12], my Secretary of War, concerning her only son, a college boy, who had enlisted in a Confederate regiment, was wounded, and taken north as a prisoner. She was seeking his release on parole from a Union hospital. When he refused, she left sobbing and found her way to see me.

"Well, Madam, are you the unhappy mother of this wounded and imprisoned son? Do you believe your boy will honor his parole if I permit him to go with you? – Then you shall have your boy my dear Madam, for to take him from the ranks of rebellion and give him to his loyal mother, is a better investment for this country than to give him up to its deadly enemy! Here, take this card! Give it to the Commanding Officer there at Fort McHenry[13]. God grant that your boy may yet prove a blessing to you, and an honor to his country[14]!"

A father and mother had come to see me concerning the return of their two boys back home. It appeared as though the boys, both underage, had enlisted in the Union Navy. The worst fault of the boys though, the parents told me, was their disobedience in joining in the first place. Well, I picked up a card and addressed it to Mr. Gideon Welles[15], Secretary of the Navy, ordering their discharge. I said, "The United States cannot afford the services of boys who disregard their parents!"

General Ambrose E. Burnside[16], upon assuming command, marched his army southward to Virginia, where he promptly lost 12,000 men at Fredericksburg[17]. He was so humiliated, that he asked to be relieved of command, - and I obliged!

I guess it was in January of this year, that I sent a letter to General Hooker[18]:

"General, I am giving you command of the Army of the Potomac! I have heard that you have said that what this army needs and what this government needs is a dictator. It is not for this, but in spite of this, that I'm giving you command. Only generals who are successful in battle can set up dictators. What I'm asking of you now is military success, and I will risk the dictatorship! Go forward and bring us victory!"

Well, General Hooker thought his plans were perfect, and he announced that when he began to carry them out, "… may God have mercy on General Lee, for he would have none!" But "General Fighting Joe Hooker," as he was called, like General Burnside, lasted but one battle, going down to major defeat at Chancellorsville[19], losing 17,000 men as Lee routed our demoralized Union forces!

"Is this the news from Chancellorsville? My God! My God! What will the country say? When I think of the sacrifices yet to be offered, and the hearts and homes of those yet to be made desolate before this dreadful war is ended, my heart is like lead within me and I feel like hiding in a deep darkness!"

Pardon me while I sign these commissions. Oh yes, this one here is for Billy Patterson[20]. Billy Patterson is a small time Mississippi River pilot, right smart though at running past Confederate batteries. He asked to be made Captain of a small Mississippi River boat sheeted with iron and mounted with two antique guns. To determine his qualifications, some pompous committee began to question Billy Patterson concerning his knowledge of English history in general, and his knowledge of Oliver Cromwell in particular. Well, Billy Patterson responded to these questions and said, "Gentlemen, I don't know who this Oliver Cromwell is, and I don't give a damn, I ain't a hunting his job!" Well, as you can see, the committee wrote upon his application, "Not recommended, ignorant and insolent!" Having reviewed this matter, it appears to me that this is a contest between Billy Patterson – and Oliver Cromwell. Since as far as I know, Oliver Cromwell is dead, - I think I can safely give this commission to Billy Patterson.

You see these papers here? These are cases they call, "Cowardice in the Face of the Enemy Cases." I call them my "Leg Cases." If Almighty God gives a man a cowardly pair of legs, I don't know how he can help but run away with them. Oh, I know I'm "pigeon hearted," even so I try to do my duty as I see it! But I must admit that after a hard day's work, it gives me some comfort if I can find some excuse to save some poor fellow's life![21]

As President and Commander in Chief, I felt a great responsibility for the army. I often thought it important that I go out to the troops, review the troops, and have a talk with my commanders. [22]On one such occasion. I had gone out to Fredericksburg to review the troops and have a talk with General McClellan. Enroute, I passed by a house that was filled with Confederate wounded. I asked to stop and go inside. Inside I told the Confederates that I would be glad to take them by the hand if they had no objection.

"Although we are enemies through uncontrollable circumstances, I hold you no malice, and I can take you by the hand with sympathy and good feeling!" After a brief pause, each Confederate able to do so came forward, and without words shook my hand. Most were moved to tears!

On another occasion as I was going out again to visit the troops and talk to my commanders, my son Tad [23] went with me. It was decided, for safety reasons, that we would go out to the troops in an ambulance driven by six mules. Throughout the eight-mile trip over rough and rugged roads, the driver was constantly cursing and shouting violent oaths as the wild mules jolted us all around the inside of that ambulance. When we arrived, I went up to the driver and said, "Excuse me my friend, are you an Episcopalian? I thought you must be an Episcopalian because you swear just like Mr. Seward[24], my Secretary of State. He is a good Episcopal Church Warden, you know. Well, the driver looked up at me and smiled and said, "No, Mr. President, I'm a Methodist!" A true story!

Well Tad, on that occasion, wanted to see some Confederate soldiers, so I thought I might oblige him by having two staff men take us early one frosty morning up to the picket lines across the river there from Fredericksburg. There in the distance a flag flew briefly in a breeze from a house, and I gazed for one of the few times upon the Confederate Stars and Bars.

Two Confederate soldiers stood silently by a tall chimney. About that time, a Confederate officer came up to the riverbank, pulled out his field glasses and peered across in our direction. He struck an attitude of dignity, pulled off his hat, made a long sweeping bow, and then retired. Well, I don't know whether that Confederate officer recognized this tall lankly form of the President of the United States and Commander in Chief of the Northern Army, but I like to think that he did!

Among the visitors who came to see me early this year, was a Brigadier General by the name of John Thayer[25].

John Thayer was from the Western Command, and originally came from Nebraska which I thought was unusual, since I thought that all the "Thayers" were from here in the East. So, I invited him in, and we chatted for about an hour.

"Come in General! Have a seat here! General, I understand you have recently come from Vicksburg! You have a man out there by the name of Grant [26]do you not? - Well, what kind of fellow is he? - Does Grant ever get drunk? - Is he in the habit of using liquor? – Well, I'm glad to hear that, because I understand that he is a good commander with a determination to win battles."

Well, despite these assurances, I continued to hear reports concerning General Grant and his drinking. On one such occasion, when I was being pushed by a gentleman to remove General Grant from command out West by reason of his drinking, I responded in this way:

"Sir, do you know what brand of liquor General Grant drinks? For if you do, I will order the Chief Quartermaster to lay in a large supply of the same kind of liquor and order him to distribute it to my other Generals who have not yet known victory! You see, what I need, and what this country needs, are commanders who can fight battles and bring us victory! I shall think further on this General Grant!"

In June of this year, General Lee [27]was determined to bring the war into the North, and he march his army from Virginia, across Maryland and on up into Pennsylvania. I had replaced General Hooker with a new commander, General George Gordon Meade.[28] General Meade, upon receiving command, promptly marched his army to meet this Rebel challenge! On July 1st, the two great armies met in a little country town there in Pennsylvania by the name of "Gettysburg"! There, after three days of very bloody battles, and over 50,000 casualties on both sides, General Lee's broken and defeated army began its retreat back to Virginia. I sent a message to General Meade, I said, "Pursue Lee's army! Do not let them escape!" But Meade hesitated, allowing General Lee's retreating forces to safely cross the Potomac River!

"We had them within our grasp! All we had to do was reach out our hands and they were ours! I'm afraid I have not yet found the commander I need to win this war and to bring us victory, but who among my generals is any better than Meade?"

You see the Capital[29] building there?" I know I have been criticized for spending the money and allowing the work on the Capital dome to continue as this war goes on, but I think it's important for the people of this country to realize that this government continues, with the confidence that this nation will still be here when this war has ended!

Early last month I received an invitation to say a few appropriate remarks at the dedication of a new National Cemetery there in Gettysburg. Mr. Edward Everett[30], a most notable orator of the day, was to be the principal speaker. But I thought I might say a few words about the greater meaning of the war, now in its third year. I had begun working on my speech here in Washington and had not yet concluded as I rode the special train to Gettysburg the day before the ceremony. That evening I continued to work on my speech, and the following morning after breakfast I added the final touches. I had written my speech on two pieces of lined paper. It was a short, short speech! That morning I rode on horseback out to the cemetery on the outskirts of Gettysburg. There, with politicians, dignitaries, brass bands, and soldiers, we paraded across the battlefield where dead horses still lay stiffly on their sides among scattered autumn leaves some four months after the battle. A crowd of some 15,000 people had assembled before the speaker's platform. Mr. Everett spoke for two hours. When it was my turn,

I left my seat, took the notes from my pocket, adjusted my spectacles, and began:

"Four score and seven years ago our fathers brought forth on this continent a new nation, conceived in Liberty, and dedicated to the proposition that all men are created equal. Now we are engaged in a great civil war, testing whether that nation or any nation so conceived and so dedicated, can long endure. We are met upon a great battlefield of that war. We have come to dedicate a portion of that field, as the final resting place for those who gave their lives that that nation might live. It is altogether fitting and proper that we should do so.

But, in a larger sense, we cannot dedicate - we cannot consecrate - we cannot hollow - this ground. The brave men, living and dead, who have struggled here, have consecrated it, far above our poor power to add or detract. The world will little note, nor long remember what we say here, but it can never forget what they did here. It is for us the living, rather, to be dedicated here to the unfinished work which they who fought here have thus far so nobly advanced. It is rather for us to be here dedicated to the great task remaining before us – that from these honored dead we take increased devotion to that cause for which they gave the last full measure of devotion – that we here highly resolve that these dead shall not have died in vain – that this nation, under God, shall have a new birth of freedom – and that government of the people, by the people, and for the people shall not perish from the earth."

When I began my speech, a photographer began to set up his equipment in order to take my photograph. I'm afraid that by the time he had gotten his camera ready, my speech had ended. It had lasted only about two minutes. I thought my speech was a failure! Mr. Everett was kind enough to write to me the following day though and say that he would have been glad enough if he could have touched on the central idea of the occasion as well in two hours, as I did in my brief two minutes of speaking!

Well, the year is drawing to a close. I don't know what the new year will bring. As for this year, I know I have not yet found the commander I need to bring us an end to this war and bring us victory. But I'm thinking now seriously on General Grant. General Grant has won victories out west in Vicksburg and more recently in Chattanooga. He's moving his army now to Georgia. Maybe there will be an end to this war! Of course, there will continue to be talk of assassination. I know I'm in danger, but I'm not going to worry about it. And in this coming year, I'm sure there will be a new election. I don't even know whether or not my Party will renominate me as its candidate for President, and if they do, I have some serious doubts as to whether or not I could be reelected! But we'll see what the new year brings!

Oh yes, Mr. Hay[31], I'm going to walk over to the War Department to check on some telegrams[32]. If you would be so kind as to take care of our guests here, and please lower the lights when they leave!

I bid you all a good evening!

Figure 1. Stephen A. Douglas

Figure 2. George McClellan

Figure 1. General Burnside

Figure 2. General Hooker

Figure 3. General Meade

Figure 6. General Ulysses S. Grant

Figure 7. General Robert E. Lee

Figure 8. General J.E.B. Stuart

Figure 9. General John Thayer

Figure 4. Gideon Wells

Figure 5. William Seward

Figure 12. Edward Stanton

Figure 6. Lincoln and McClellan at Antietam

Figure 14. Lincoln and McClellan in Tent

Figure 15. "Tad" Lincoln

Figure 7. Edward Everett

Figure 17. Billy Herndon

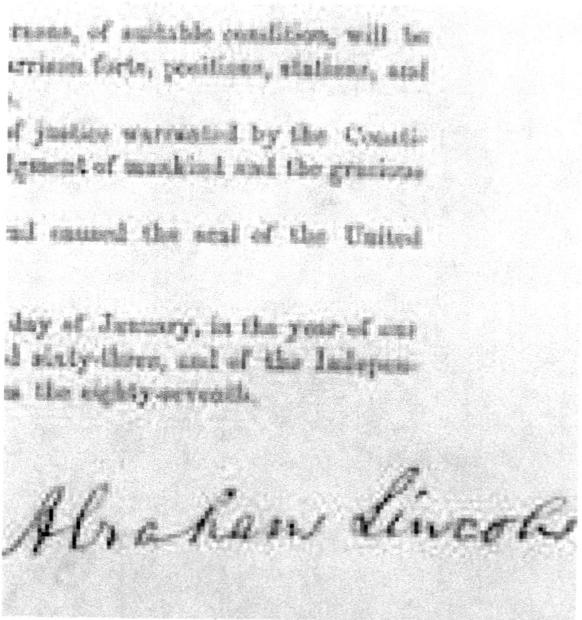

rsons, of suitable condition, will be
garrison forts, positions, stations, and

of justice warranted by the Consti-
gment of mankind and the gracious

and caused the seal of the United

day of January, in the year of our
d sixty-three, and of the Indepen-
n the eighty-seventh.

Abraham Lincoln

Figure 8. Signature Page Emancipation Proclamation

Figure 9. Capital Building

Figure 10. John Hay

Epilog

Some of those telegrams that Lincoln would go to the War Office to see still contained news of hard fighting and heavy casualties. But there was also hope in the air as well.

The war would continue for almost two more years and Lincoln was still looking for a commander to head the Union Army and bring victories and an end to the war. It would not be until March of 1864 that Lincoln would find that commander in the form of Ulysses S. Grant, and name him to that position.

There would still be great losses and defeats, but there would also be Union victories, and the Union forces would eventually wear down and force the surrender of the outnumbered and under equipped Confederate armies.

Lincoln would receive his party's nomination for a second term and in a close election in 1865, Lincoln would defeat George McClellan, his former Commanding General, for reelection to the office of President of the United States.

With the news of the surrender of General Lee and his army at Appomattox on April 9, 1865, the end of the war appeared at hand. The nation had survived and had been victorious.

"With malice toward none, with charity for all," Lincoln laid plans for a generous reconstruction program that would bring the seceded states back into the Union.

But on Good Friday, April 14, 1865, while attending a performance of "Our American Cousin" at the Ford's Theater in Washington D.C., Abraham Lincoln was assassinated. The following morning at 7:22 A. M., the 16th President of the United States died at fifty-six years of age.

At the moment of Lincoln's death, Secretary of War, Edwin M. Stanton [33]murmured, "Now he belongs to the ages!"

Figure 11. Don Germano portraying Lincoln

Endnotes

The following Endnotes and additional information presented here on some of the individuals and events mentioned in Lincoln's talk have been gathered from various sources including Wikipedia.

---

[1] **Stephen A. Douglas,** nicknamed the "Little Giant," was a lawyer, judge, politician, and member of the Democratic Party. He won reelection as U.S. Senator from the State of Illinois against Lincoln in 1858. He ran for President and lost to Lincoln for that office in 1860. He died in office as a United States Senator the following year.

[2] **The "House Divided Speech"** was delivered by Lincoln on June 16, 1858, in Springfield, Illinois at the State Convention of the Republican Party after he had accepted the party's nomination for U.S. Senator from the State of Illinois. Lincoln lost the election, but the speech helped to bring him national prominence, and afterwards, he was considered as a potential candidate for President of the United States.

[3] **The Lincoln – Douglas Debates** were seven debates between Lincoln, the Republican candidate, and Stephen A. Douglas, the Democratic candidate, for the seat from the State of Illinois to the United States Senate, held between August and October of 1858. The speeches focused on slavery. Douglas spoke for local sovereignty with the new states deciding for themselves the issue of slavery. Lincoln argued against

the existence of slavery in the new states. Douglas was re-elected by vote of the Illinois General Assembly 54 – 46.

[4]**William (Bill) Henry Herndon** was a lawyer and younger law partner of Abraham Lincoln. He was a member of the newly formed Republican Party and was later elected Mayor of Springfield, Illinois. Lincoln once said Herndon, "was my man, always above all other men on the globe." But Herndon was never invited to Lincoln's home in Springfield or to the private living quarters of the White House due to his contentious relationship with Mary Todd Lincoln.

[5]**Grace Bedell (Billings)** is remembered for her letter, as an eleven-year-old girl from New York, to Lincoln, then the Republican nominee for President of the United States. She encouraged Lincoln to grow a beard. He did, and on his way by train from Springfield to Washington for his inauguration as the 16th President of the United States, Lincoln's train stopped in Westfield, New York, and there Lincoln met and talked with young Grace Bedell. He kissed her on the cheek and showed her his beard. She never saw him again.

[6] **Lincoln's "Farewell Address"** was delivered by Lincoln, as the newly elected President, to the people of his hometown, Springfield, Illinois, on February 11, 1861. Lincoln spoke from the back of his private train as he was about to depart on his way from Springfield to Washington for his inauguration as the 16th President of the United States. Hundreds of citizens of Springfield gathered there at the train station in the rain

to wish Lincoln well and to see him off to his destiny. This "Farewell Address" is remembered as one of Lincoln's most emotional speeches.

[7]**George B. McClellan** was a Union General during the Civil War. He served as Commanding General of the United States Army from November 1861 to March of 1862 when Lincoln removed him from command, but he continued to serve as Commander of the Army of the Potomac until November of 1862. Lincoln and McClellan had a mutual distrust for each other, and McClellan was often disrespectful of Lincoln, his Commander in Chief. McClellan became the unsuccessful Democratic Party's nominee in the 1864 Presidential election against Abraham Lincoln. After the war, McClellan was elected Governor of New Jersey. He later wrote his memoirs, "McClellan's Own Story," published posthumously in 1887.

[8] **J.E.B. Stuart** was a Confederate General from Virginia during the Civil War. He was a Cavalry Commander, noted for his colorful dress, a red lined grey cape, yellow waist sash, hat cocked to the side with an ostrich plume, red flower in his lapel, and often wearing cologne. He was an expert in reconnaissance and General Lee considered him his "eyes and ears" of the army. But at Gettysburg, his long delay from the battle left Lee unaware of the position of the Union troops, resulting in Lee being surprised and disadvantaged at the three-day Battle of Gettysburg. During the 1864 Overland Campaign, "Jeb" Stuart was surprised, shot in the face, and mortally wounded at the Battle of Yellow Tavern by a member of General Phil Sheridan's Union Cavalry.

[9] **Stuart's Chambersburg Raid** was a raid by "JEB" Stuart's Calvary around Chambersburg, Pennsylvania, October 10-12, 1862. General Lee had ordered the raid for the purpose of reconnaissance and for needed supplies through Maryland and Pennsylvania. The raid was successful. It was Stuart's second ride around McClellan's Union forces and contributed to Lincoln's later removal of McClellan as Commander of the Army of the Potomac in November of 1862.

[10]**Lincoln and Slavery.** Lincoln's first impression of slavery was as a child in Kentucky. His mother and father belonged to a small company of Abolitionist. So evil did they hold slavery, that they were willing to leave their home in Kentucky and to move to Illinois, a "free state." There Lincoln did not see many slaves, and it was not until he made his first flat bottomed boat trip down the Mississippi River to New Orleans as a young man of 19 years of age that he began to see them in large numbers. But it was on his second trip to New Orleans three years later that he saw Negroes chained, maltreated, whipped, and scourged, and Lincoln's heart bled for these fellow human beings and then and there he formed his opinion against the evils of slavery.

[11]**The Emancipation Proclamation** was an Executive Order originally signed by President Lincoln on September 22, 1862 but was formerly signed and became effective on January 1, 1863. The legal effect was to free more than 3.5 million slaves in the ten secessionist Confederate States. It further permitted them to "be received into the Armed Forces of the United States." The Proclamation gave hope to the enslaved population of America. It had the effect also

of discouraging any European entry into the Civil War on the side of the Confederacy, and it redefined the Civil War, turning it from a struggle to preserve the Union to one focused on ending slavery.

[12]**Edwin M. Stanton** was a lawyer and politician who originally opposed Lincoln but became a part of Lincoln's Cabinet and served as his Secretary of War. Stanton became one of Lincoln's closest advisers. After Lincoln's assassination, Stanton helped to organize the manhunt for Lincoln's assassin, John Wilkes Booth. He remained as Secretary of War under President Andrew Johnson but opposed Johnson's harsh policies toward the former Confederate States.

[13]**Fort McHenry** on the shores of Baltimore, Maryland was a Union Fort and Federal Hospital during the Civil War. Previously, in 1814, during the Battle of Baltimore with the British, Francis Scott Key, seeing the stars and stripes of the American flag still flying during the bombardment of the Fort, was inspired to write the "Star- Bangled Banner" which became the American National Anthem.

[14] **The Prisoner Exchange Program,** codified on July 22, 1862, by the Dix Hill Cartel, called for equal exchange of all captured soldiers, who could then return to their units to fight further battles. But large-scale prisoner exchange ceased by August of 1863, which resulted in a dramatic increase in prisoner population, often with deplorable conditions on both sides for the remainder of the Civil War.

[15]**Gideon Wells** was a politician from the State of Connecticut who had supported Lincoln for the Presidency. For this support, Lincoln appointed him to serve as his Secretary of the Navy during the Civil War, and he continued to serve in that capacity until 1869. Although personally opposed to the blockade of southern ports during the Civil War, he nonetheless carried out that policy, sealing the Confederate coastline from receiving needed war supplies. This has been viewed by historians as a major cause of the ultimate Union victory.

[16]**General Ambrose E. Burnside** was appointed by President Lincoln to replace General McClellan on November 5, 1862, after the Battles of Sharpsburg and Antietam, and he then assumed command of the Army of the Potomac. In his first battle as Commander, Burnside suffered a major defeat for the Union forces at Fredericksburg on December 13, 1862, where he was labeled, "the Butcher of Fredericksburg", and resigned his commission. Later in the war, in command of an Army Corps at Petersburg, Virginia, he again suffered a major defeat for the Union forces at the Battle of the Crater, July 30, 1863. As a result, he was placed on "extended leave" by General Grant, relieved of command, and was never recalled for the remainder of the war. After the war, Burnside served three terms as Governor of the State of Rhode Island and later as U.S. Senator from that State. Burnside is still remembered today for his spectacular growth of what became known as "sideburns," a name derived from the two parts of his name.

[17]**The Battle of Fredericksburg** was fought in Fredericksburg, Virginia on December 11-13, 1862, between Union and Confederate forces. It was one of the most one-sided battles of the Civil War. The Union forces under General Burnside delivered repeated frontal attacks on the entrenched Confederate forces led by General Robert E. Lee, resulting in Union casualties of over 12,000 men, twice that of the Confederate army.

[18]**Joseph Hooker,** Union General during the Civil War distinguished himself at Williamsburg, Antietam, and Fredericksburg. Upon General Burnside being relieved of command of the Union Army of the Potomac, Hooker, was named as his replacement. "Fighting Joe Hooker," as he was called, had ambitious plans for defeating General Lee at Chancellorsville, but was severely "out generaled," resulting in the routing of a Union Corps and over 17,000 Union casualties. This defeat encouraged General Lee to move his army north toward Gettysburg. When General Hooker was refused enforcements, he resigned three days before the Battle of Gettysburg. General Hooker's personal reputation was as a "ladies' man," a hard drinker known for partying and gambling. His name, "Hooker" became a slang term for prostitutes not only because of his wild parties, but also for his lack of moral military discipline, allowing his troops to be exposed to the favors of such women.

[19]**The Battle of Chancellorsville** was fought there in Virginia over a period of seven days beginning April 30, 1863. The newly appointed Joseph Hooker's Union forces faced the Confederate forces of General Robert

E. Lee which resulted in a serious Union defeat and over 17.000 Union casualties. For Lee, it was deemed a "perfect battle," with Lee's risky decision of dividing his army in the face of Hooker's much larger force resulting in a significant Confederate victory. But the Confederates suffered major casualties as well. (Over 12,000, 22 per cent of Lee's forces, including the loss of General "Stonewall" Jackson to friendly fire, a loss that Lee likened to "losing his right arm").

[20]**Billy Patterson** was only one of 6,700 Union Naval officers at the end of the Civil War. The control of the Mississippi River was a major goal of the Union Navy throughout the Civil War with the intention of cutting the Confederacy in two and denying them easy access to transportation of troops, weapons, and supplies. Its control contributed heavily to the ultimate Union victory over the Confederacy. At least sixty-three little gunboats dubbed, "tinclads," were converted from small steamboats and riverboats on the Mississippi River by the addition of boilerplate armor. Although not a part of any major engagements, as in the battles for New Orleans or Memphis, these "tinclads" nevertheless made major contributions to the Union operations and ultimate success on the Mississippi River. They served to bypass and sometimes reduce Confederate batteries, engaged rebel sharpshooters, and carried needed weapons and supplies to Union troops.

[21]**Pardon Power of the President:** During his Presidency, President Lincoln exercised the Presidential power to pardon on numerous occasions. After thoughtful consideration of over 1,600 cases,

Lincoln would pardon a number of soldiers condemned to die for cowardice in the face of the enemy, desertion, or sleeping on duty. Although he would do his duty as President and Commander in Chief of the Armed Forces, Lincoln would show mercy and compassion whenever he could justify such action on his part.

[22]**Lincoln's Field Trips.** Lincoln often conferred with his field commanders, usually by telegraph, but also in person at the White House, and often went to visit them in the field. He visited General McClellan on October 3, 1862, at Antietam, Maryland, and it was there that Alexander Gardner made his well-known photographs of that meeting of President Lincoln and General McClellan and members of his staff in the field.

[23]**Thomas (Tad) Lincoln** was the youngest child of Abraham and Mary Todd Lincoln. He was given the name, "Tad," by his father because he had a somewhat large head and was as "wiggly as a tadpole." Tad had a free run of the White House and was a favorite of his father who often took him as he travelled. Tad Lincoln survived his father and lived to the age of eighteen when he suddenly died of an unspecified illness.

[24]**William Henry Seward** was Lincoln's Secretary of State. He had been a member of the newly formed Republican Party and ran unsuccessfully against Lincoln for the office of President of the United States in 1860. Seward was named by Lincoln to his Cabinet as Secretary of State in December of that year, and in that capacity was successful in preventing the French

from supporting and recognizing the Confederacy in the Civil War. As part of the plot to assassinate President Lincoln, Steward was attacked by Lewis Powell, a co-conspirator of John Wilkes Booth, and was stabbed in the face and throat and narrowly survived. He later served other administrations as a diplomat and was instrumental in the purchase of Alaska, (Seward's Folly) from Russia in 1867.

[25]**John Thayer** was born in Massachusetts but moved his family out west at the age of 34. He was an active Republican in the Nebraska Territory, a Delegate to its Convention for Statehood, and a Major General in the Territorial Militia. In response to Lincoln's call for volunteers in 1861, Thayer joined the Union Army. He was promoted to the rank of Brigadier General and spent the entire war fighting in the Western Command under General Grant, including at Shiloh, Fort Donelson, and the siege of Vicksburg. After the war, when Nebraska became a State, Thayer was elected as a U. S. Senator from that State. President Grant later appointed Thayer as Governor of the Territory of Wyoming. He served two terms as Governor of Nebraska. A bust of General Thayer is located on the grounds of the Vicksburg National Military Park in Mississippi.

[26]**Ulysses S. Grant** was born in Ohio, attended West Point, and upon graduation became an officer in the United States Army, serving with distinction in the Mexican American War. In 1843 he joined the Union Army and when the Civil War broke out he rose in rank after several Union victories in the Western Theater. In 1863 he led the Vicksburg Campaign, winning victory

there and then in Chattanooga, after which President Lincoln placed him at the head of the Union Army. General Lee surrendered to him at Appomattox on April 9, 1865. As a war hero Grant was unanimously nominated by the Republican Party as its candidate for President and was elected as the 18th President of the United States in 1868, serving two terms. After retirement, he was the first President to circumnavigate the world on his world tour. In July of 1885 Grant finished his memories and died a few weeks later of throat cancer at the age of sixty-three.

[27] **General Robert E. Lee** was a Virginian who became the Commanding General of the Confederate forces during the Civil War. He had attended West Point where he was among the top of his class and thereafter entered his 34-year military career. He fought with distinction and won a reputation as a good tactician and officer in the Mexican American War. As an Officer in the U.S. Army, he led an assault on the Abolitionist John Brown at Harper's Ferry. Brown had hoped to incite a slave uprising, but Lee's assault ended in Brown's capture and later execution. When the Civil War broke out, Lee was offered Command of the Union Army, but turned down the offer in loyalty to his native State of Virginia which had joined the Confederacy. At the beginning of the Civil War, Lee served as military advisor to Jefferson Davis, President of the Confederacy. In June of 1862, however, Lee was named Commanding General of the Army of Northern Virginia, after which he had major and decisive military victories over the Union forces including those at Fredericksburg, Chancellorsville and elsewhere. His hopes of winning the war by a

successful invasion of the North was ended with the decisive defeat of his Confederate forces by those of the Union Army at Gettysburg. Although the war continued for almost two more years with the Confederate forces under General Lee's command, after the capture of Richmond by the Union forces and the destruction of most of Lee's Confederate forces, Lee was forced to surrender his army to General Grant at Appomattox in April of 1865. Following the war, Lee became President of the college that later became known as Washington and Lee. Robert E. Lee died on October 12, 1870. Lee has been called the "winning-most General" of the Civil War.

[28] **George Gordon Meade** was born in Spain. He became a Union General during the Civil War. He was considered to be the most successful Union Commander at the Battle of Fredericksburg. He was promoted to Major General in charge of the Union Army of the Potomac just three days before the Battle of Gettysburg and there defeated General Lee's Confederate forces in a decisive defensive battle. This ended Lee's hopes of winning the war through a successful invasion of the North. Meade was discredited, however, when he failed to follow up his Union victory at Gettysburg and allowed Lee's army to safety cross the Potomac River and to return back to Virginia to fight more battles before the war was ended.

[29] **The Dome of the Capital Building** was under construction throughout the Civil War and was not finished until 1866. The Statute of Freedom placed on

top of the Capital in December of 1863 had been originally designed and selected by Jefferson Davis (President of the Confederacy), prior to the Civil War when Davis was Secretary of War under President Franklin Pierce.

[30]**Edward Everet**t was an educator, politician, and orator from the State of Massachusetts, best known for delivering a two-hour speech at Gettysburg immediately before Lincoln delivered his shorter two minute "Gettysburg Address". Before this, Everett had taught at Harvard and served as its President. When he became interested in politics, he served ten years in Congress, as Minister to Great Britain, Governor of Massachusetts, Secretary of State for a short while, and as a U.S. Senator. He ran unsuccessfully as a Vice-Presidential candidate on the Constitutional Union Party in 1860 against Lincoln's Republican Party ticket. He supported the Union during the Civil War and became a well-known orator during the war speaking on behalf of the Union. He supported Lincoln during his run for a second term as President in 1864.

[31]**John Hay** had read law in his uncle's law office next to that of Abraham Lincoln in Springfield, Illinois. He had worked on Lincoln's Presidential campaign and after Lincoln's election, became Lincoln's personal secretary in the White House. He was by the bed when Lincoln died. He remained in politics after Lincoln's death and became Secretary of State under President McKinley and Theodore Roosevelt. In that capacity, he helped clear the way for the building of the Panama Canal.

[32]**Lincoln's Use of the Telegraph**. Lincoln had a keen interest in technology and would embrace the telegraph, newly invented by Samuel B. Morse. Lincoln spent more time of his Presidency in the War Department's telegraph office than anywhere else outside the White House. He visited there several times a day and every night before turning in, often sleeping there on a cot during major battles, peering over the shoulders of the operators as the "lightening messages," as he called them, came in. He would follow the progress of the war and communicate with his commanders, often suggesting courses of action.

.